AF576559

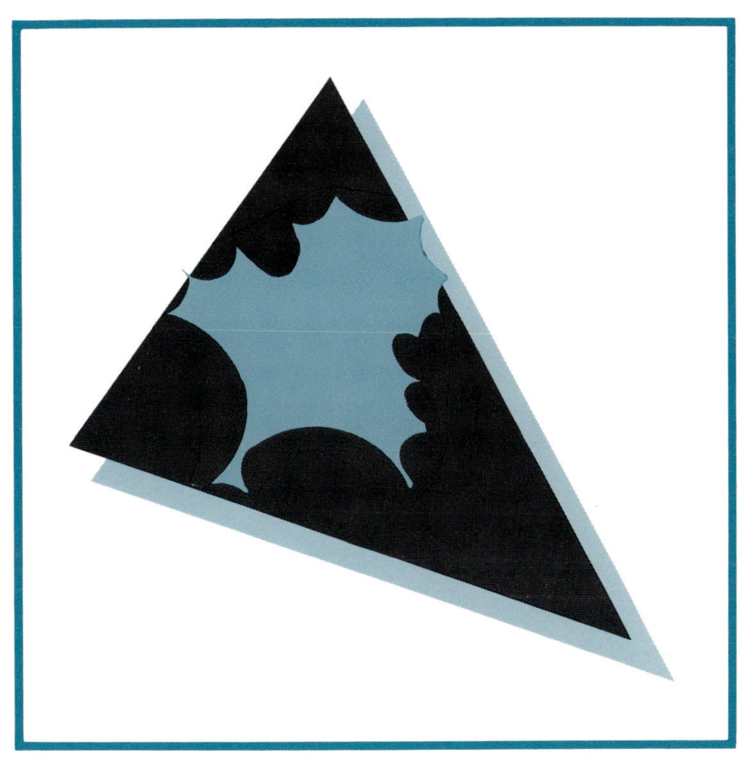

P.O. Box 13819, 8112 W. Bluemound Road
Milwaukee, WI 53213 U.S.A.

ISBN 0-88188-422-7
HL 00183535
Library of Congress Catalog Card Number
85-82268
Printed in the U.S.A.

Produced & edited by J. Aaron Brown,
Isabel D. Landeo & David R. Lehman

Designed by Teresa Towery

Typeset by Karen Perry

All articles written by Kelly DeLaney

A J. Aaron Brown & Associates Publication
in association with

THE BOOK OF WORDS

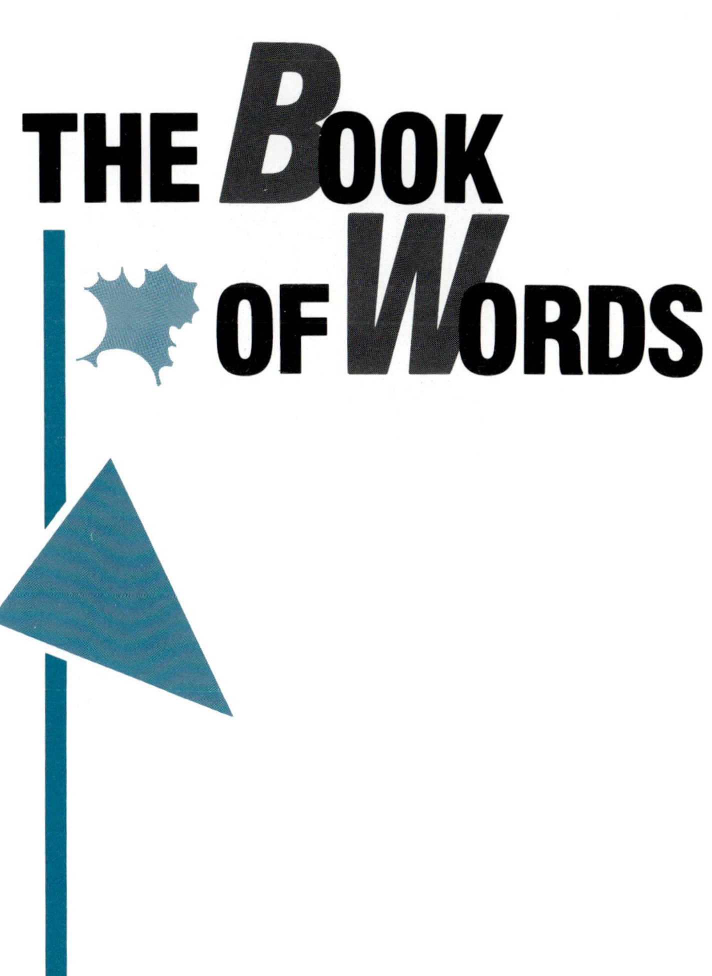

Don Putnam

PHOTOGRAPHY

Tom Edwards (35), J. Frey (39), Harrison Funk (Cover), Beth Gwinn (73), Annie Leibovitz (28, 34, 39, 40, 43, 44, 46, 47, 48, 49, 70, 80), Kathy McClintock (43), Alan Messer (10, 15, 33, 37, 38, 40, 42, 43, 46, 47, 48, 71, 72, 75, 77), Jon Mir (40), Rick Norton (56), Hope Powell (74), Don Putnam (4, 35, 41, 56, 70, 73, 74, 76), Norman Seeff (32), Randee St. Nicholas (35, 36, 39, 43, 47), Raul Vega (45).

Cover photograph by HARRISON FUNK, © 1985

CONTENTS

THE SONGWORDS INDEX

Mr. Duane Allen
329 Rockland Road
Hendersonville, TN 37075

Dear Duane,

I've given some more thought to "The Book of Words" idea. I want the book to somehow reflect the deep relationship that exists between The Oak Ridge Boys and their songs. This collection of lyrics would illustrate The Oaks' sincere commitment to recording only the greatest songs.

Duane, I have enclosed a list of songs that express that feeling. Look over the list and add to it as you see fit. I would also like for each of you to share your personal impressions about some of the lyrics and what they have come to mean to you.

Please give this some thought and get back in touch.

Soon,

J. Aaron Brown

P.S. Keep recording great songs.

1508 Sixteenth Avenue South • Nashville, Tennessee 37212 USA • 615/385-0022

Mastercraft Music • Prime Time Music • Snowfox Music

Dear Aaron,

Since the Oaks individually did not write any of our hits in this collection, most of our experiences with each song came with the performance of the song.

I remember well when we began to sing "Thank God for Kids". Within our group, we were going through a difficult period of time. "Thank God for Kids" encouraged us to lay aside our complicated adult problems and gently approach our problems through the eyes of a child. I believe this ultimately caused each of us to build a broader capacity of caring and understanding of each others feelings.

Each song has a story and every ong builds many memories. I hope these tories and memories will make you smile you see each song title.

Duane

329 Rockland Road • Hendersonville, TN 37075 • (615) 824-492

THE MIGHTY OAKS

By Kelly DeLaney

The four present day Oak Ridge Boys—William Lee Golden, Duane Allen, Richard Sterban and Joe Bonsall are carrying on a musical tradition of excellence and innovation which began over 40 years ago during World War II.

Back then, the tiny community of Oak Ridge, located in east central Tennessee, was the site of the top secret Manhattan Project which culminated in the construction of the world's first atom bomb.

A group of four singers and a piano accompanist, then known as the Country Cutups frequently entertained the local residents and government employees who lived in Oak Ridge. Perhaps, due in part to the perilous nature of the times, the group found that audiences responded best to its Southern styled gospel music repertoire.

Following the war, the group by now having undergone a name change to the Oak Ridge Quartet, relocated in Nashville. There, its leader, Wally Fowler, initiated the all night gospel singings on November 5, 1948, at Ryman Auditorium. This event is significant because it began a tradition of trendsetting which has continued throughout The Oak Ridge Boy's illustrious career.

The quartet disbanded briefly in 1956, but reformed in 1957 under the direction of Smitty Gatlin. This unit expanded on the trendsetting tradition, according to Herman Harper, the quartet's bass singer from 1957 to 1968.

"We were the first gospel group ever to wear turtle neck sweaters," he recalls. "We even had some dates cancelled because of it. No one ever knew what we were going to do next."

The group recorded two noteworthy albums for Warner Brothers Records, the first one resulting in the alteration of the name from "Quartet" to "Boys". Harper explains that record company executives thought that "Quartet" sounded too old

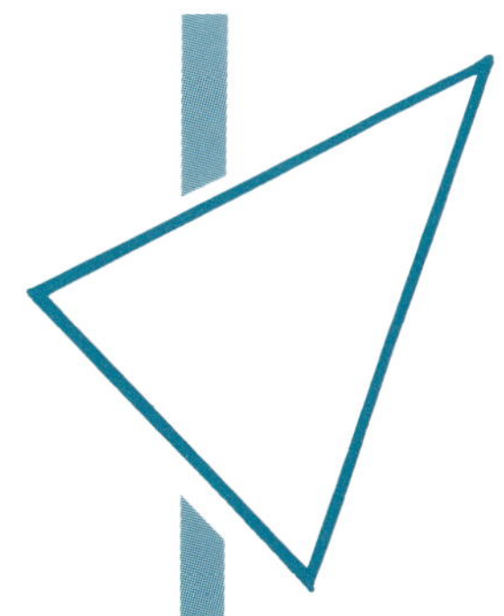

fashioned, and since the group's members were all young, they deemed "Boys" more appropriate.

Their debut album on Warner Brothers Records - "The Oak Ridge Boys With Sounds Of Nashville" was the first gospel album ever recorded with strings and horns.

During the height of the folk music era, the Oaks recorded their second album for that label entitled, "Folk Minded Folks," which featured primarily acoustic instruments.

The first of the present members to join the group was William Lee Golden in 1964. "When the baritone position came open, Smitty hired him," Harper says, "And boy, was he ready to go!"

"I had heard the group a lot," Golden remembers. "I thought they were the most exciting group I had ever heard. Becoming an Oak Ridge Boy was the most important thing in the world to me."

Two years later, in 1966 Duane Allen joined as the lead singer. "I took over as manager when Smitty left the group, and I hired Duane," Harper says. "We knew what a great singer he was."

Like Golden, Allen was an Oaks' fan long before he was a member of the group. "I used to go up to Fort Worth over a period of years to see them perform," Allen adds. "I had talked with Smitty several times about joining the group someday."

Next to come aboard was Richard Sterban in 1972. Prior to becoming an Oak Ridge Boy he was a member of the Stamps Quartet and traveled with the Elvis Presley show. "I thought that out of all the

gospel groups, The Oak Ridge Boys had the most potential," Sterban relates. "So when they offered me the job as bass singer, I did not even hesitate to take it."

Bonsall, who followed Sterban in 1973, had been on shows with the Oaks while he was a tenor singer with the Keystone Quartet, a gospel group based in the northeastern United States. He and Sterban previously had sung together in that group.

The Oak Ridge Boys were known primarily for their gospel music accomplishments until 1977 when they scored their first secular hit, "Y'all Come Back Saloon". "That was our first real radio exposure," says Sterban. "That record turned the corner for us and took us from a struggling act to one with some credibility in country music."

Before the success of "Y'all Come Back Saloon" the Oaks barely managed to survive while making the transition from gospel to secular music. Ironically, the foursome's original intent was to broaden the appeal of gospel music, which they attempted to achieve with three albums on Columbia Records.

As their hair inched over their shirt collars and they hired a drummer (a practice then unheard of in gospel music), The Oak Ridge Boys became known as rebels. They

were even accused of trying to bring rock and roll into the churches. Like their musical brethren before them, the four Oaks were departing from tradition, while setting a course for the future of gospel music. In only a couple of years, the Oaks plummeted from being a successful gospel group, with 12 Dove Awards to its credit, to becoming a virtually unbookable entity which actually managed to lose $100,000 in 1976.

Since 1977 when The Oak Ridge Boys signed with ABC Records (now MCA Records) they have maintained an unbroken string of hit recordings, with the platinum-selling single, "Elvira" heading the list. This smash recording topped both the country and pop music charts.

The Oaks have belted out ten Gold Albums with two others - "Greatest Hits" and "Fancy Free" reaching Platinum and Double Platinum status respectively.

The group has been honored numerous times by the Country Music Association, the Academy of Country Music, and the Jukebox Operators of America, among many others.

There have been no changes in the group since 1973, an indication of the Oaks' solidarity and commitment to music. Bonsall expresses the group's devotion to one another: "You know, when success hit, it would have been just as easy for us to grow apart. Instead we grew closer. I'd do anything for anyone of them, and I know they'd do the same for me. It's love."

Indeed it is love - a love for music which began over 40 years ago. "I hope it goes on forever," Herman Harper offers. Beyond any doubt, William Lee Golden, Duane Allen, Richard Sterban and Joe Bonsall have made an important contribution to the music legacy of The Oak Ridge Boys. They are part of a tradition which will endure the test of time.

EVERYDAY

by Dave Loggins & J.D. Martin

YOU KNOW A SMILE NEVER GOES OUT OF STYLE
SO BRIGHTEN UP THE ONE THAT YOU WEAR
LET IT SHINE AND YOU JUST MIGHT FIND
YOU'LL LIGHTEN UP THE LOAD THAT YOU BEAR

YOU KNOW WITH ALL OF THE TROUBLE
AND SORROW IN THE WORLD
IT SEEMS LIKE THE LEAST WE CAN DO
IS TAKE THAT SMILE INTO THE STREET
AND SHARE IT WITH EVERYBODY YOU MEET

EVERYDAY (EVERYDAY)
I WANNA SHAKE SOMEBODY'S HAND
EVERYDAY (EVERYDAY)
I WANNA MAKE SOMEBODY KNOW (THAT THINKS THEY CAN)
THAT THEY CAN (YES, THEY CAN)
EVERYDAY (EVERYDAY)
I WANNA TRY (I WANNA TRY)
TO SHOW MY BROTHERS AND MY SISTERS THAT I
WANNA HELP THEM
ALONG THE WAY
EVERYDAY, EVERYDAY

YOU KNOW A KIND WORD NEVER GOES UNHEARD
BUT TOO OFTEN GOES UNSAID
AND ON THE TONGUE OF THE OLD AND THE YOUNG
IT'S SWALLOWED UP WITH PRIDE INSTEAD

YOU KNOW WITH ALL OF THE TROUBLE
AND SORROW IN THE WORLD
IT SEEMS LIKE THE LEAST WE CAN DO
IS TAKE A KIND WORD
INTO THE STREET
AND SHARE IT WITH EVERYBODY YOU MEET

EVERYDAY (EVERYDAY)
I WANNA SHAKE SOMEBODY'S HAND—(YEAH)
EVERYDAY (EVERYDAY)
I WANNA MAKE SOMEBODY KNOW (THAT THINKS THEY CAN)
THAT THEY CAN (YES, THEY CAN)
EVERYDAY (EVERYDAY)
I WANNA TRY (I WANNA TRY)
TO SHOW MY BROTHERS AND MY SISTERS THAT I
WANNA HELP THEM
ALONG THE WAY
EVERYDAY, EVERYDAY

IF THEY'RE LOST I WANNA SHOW THEM
THE SUN SHINE
IF THEY LOOK TOSSED I WANT TO THROW THEM
A LIFE LINE

I WANNA REACH OUT MY HAND
(REACH OUT) A HAND TO HOLD
AND LET THEM KNOW (LET THEM KNOW)
THERE'S A LIGHT (THERE'S A LIGHT)
DOWN AT THE END OF THE ROAD

by Steve Runkle

TELL YOU WHY I CALLED ON YOU
THIS IS WHAT WE'RE GONNA DO
TAKE THIS LOVELY GIFT OF LOVE
SENT TO US FROM HEAVEN ABOVE
I SAID, BABY
I THINK THAT WE COULD HELP EACH OTHER TO SEE
OH, YEAH
WE'D MAKE THIS LIFE THAT WE'RE LIVIN'
SEEM MORE THAN IT'S SUPPOSED TO BE

WELL, EVERY MAN SHOULD HAVE A GOOD WOMAN
EVERY WOMAN SHOULD HAVE A GOOD MAN
WON'T YOU STAND ALONG BESIDE ME
LET ME DO THE BEST I CAN
TAKE EACH OTHER'S HEART IN HAND

I WANT TO SING
JUST A LITTLE LOVE SONG
I WANT TO SING
FOR YOU A LITTLE WHILE
BACK UP AND TOE
THE LINE FOR YOU
I WANT TO BE YOUR ALL IN ALL

BLESS YOU BABY, I LOVE YOU SO
LOVE FROM WHOM ALL BLESSINGS FLOW
ME TO YOU AND YOU TO ME
THIS IS HOW IT'S GONNA BE
I SAID, BABY
WE'RE GONNA KNOW THE JOY THE YEARS CAN BRING
OH YES WE WILL
AND EVERY TIME I THINK ABOUT IT
I JUST WANT TO LIFT MY HEART AND SING
ONE MORE TIME

EVERY MAN SHOULD HAVE A GOOD WOMAN
EVERY WOMAN SHOULD HAVE A GOOD MAN
WON'T YOU STAND ALONG BESIDE ME
LET ME DO THE BEST I CAN
TAKE EACH OTHER'S HEART IN HAND

I WANT TO SING
JUST A LITTLE LOVE SONG
I WANT TO SING
FOR YOU A LITTLE WHILE
BACK UP AND TOE
THE LINE FOR YOU
I WANT TO BE YOUR ALL IN ALL IN ALL

LOVE SONG

AMERICAN MADE

by Bob Dipiero & Pat McManus

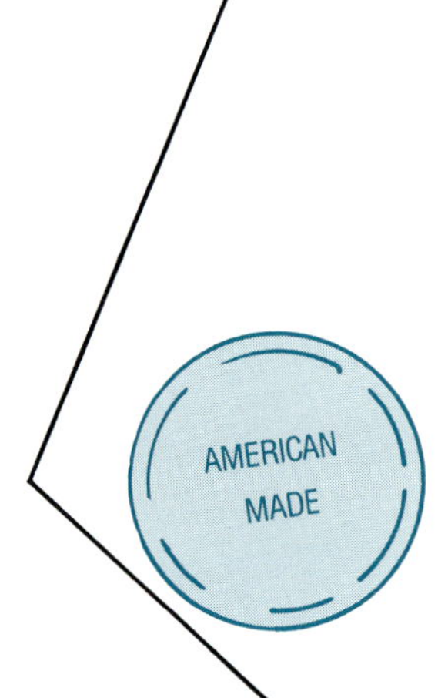

SEEMS EVERYTHING I BUY THESE DAYS
HAS GOT A FOREIGN NAME
FROM THE KIND OF CAR I DRIVE
TO MY VIDEO GAME
I'VE GOT A NIKON CAMERA
A SONY COLOR T.V.
BUT THE ONE THAT I LOVE
IS FROM THE U.S.A.
AND STANDING NEXT TO ME

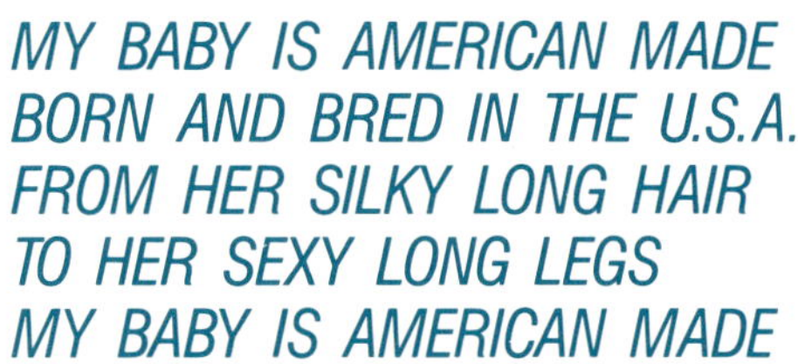

MY BABY IS AMERICAN MADE
BORN AND BRED IN THE U.S.A.
FROM HER SILKY LONG HAIR
TO HER SEXY LONG LEGS
MY BABY IS AMERICAN MADE

SHE LOOKS GOOD IN HER TIGHT BLUE JEANS
SHE BOUGHT IN MEXICO
AND SHE LOVES WEARING FRENCH PERFUME
EVERYWHERE WE GO
BUT WHEN IT COMES TO THE LOVIN' PART
ONE THING IS TRUE
MY BABY'S GENUINE U.S.A.
RED, WHITE AND BLUE

MY BABY IS AMERICAN MADE
BORN AND BRED N THE U.S.A.
FROM HER SILKY LONG HAIR
TO HER SEXY LONG LEGS
MY BABY IS AMERICAN MADE

UNTIL YOU

by Jimbeau Hinson & Rusty Golden

BABY
FEEL MY HEARTBEAT
RACING WILDLY
TO MATCH YOUR EVERY MOVE
SOMETHING YOU DO EVERY DAY
BUT IT NEVER BEAT THIS WAY
UNTIL YOU

YOUR STARE
TAKES ME OUT THERE
WHERE I DON'T CARE
ABOUT ANYTHING BUT YOU
NEVER LET NOBODY ELSE
SO DEEP INSIDE MYSELF
UNTIL YOU

UNTIL YOU
LIFE WAS GOING THROUGH THE MOTIONS
LIKE A SHIP OUT ON THE OCEAN EVER BLUE
UNTIL YOU
LOVE WAS A ONE-SIDED EMOTION
LACKING THEIR OR MY DEVOTION NEVER TRUE
UNTIL YOU

YOU FULFILL ME
YOU THRILL ME
WHEN YOU TELL ME
I'M THE ONLY ONE FOR YOU
MAKES ME WANT TO BE THE BEST
TOWER OVER ALL THE REST
JUST FOR YOU

UNTIL YOU
LIFE WAS GOING THROUGH THE MOTIONS
LIKE A SHIP OUT ON THE OCEAN EVER BLUE
UNTIL YOU
LOVE WAS A ONE-SIDED EMOTION
LACKING THEIR OR MY DEVOTION NEVER TRUE
UNTIL YOU

DREAM ON
DREAM ON

by Dennis Lambert & Brian Potter

LAY YOUR HEAD DOWN ON MY SHOULDER
I WON'T LET THE NIGHT GET COLDER
I'LL PROTECT YOU
I'LL BE KEEPIN'
TROUBLE FAR FROM WHERE YOU'RE SLEEPIN'
UNTIL YOU WAKE IN THE MORNING
YOU'VE GOT THE WORLD TO YOURSELF

DREAM ON
DREAM ABOUT THE WORLD
WE'RE GONNA LIVE IN
ONE FINE DAY
DREAM ON
SPEND THE NIGHT IN HEAVEN
I'LL BE HERE
TO LIGHT YOUR WAY
SOMEDAY TOMORROW WILL SMILE
BUT LITTLE GIRL IN THE MEANWHILE
DREAM ON

YOU'RE A PRINCESS
CHAINS AROUND YOU
I'M A HERO WHO JUST FOUND YOU
'TILL A BRAND NEW DAY MUST WAKE YOU
LET IMAGINATION TAKE YOU
GO WHERE THE MUSIC IS PLAYIN'
I'LL BE ALONG IN A WHILE

DREAM ON
DREAM ABOUT THE WORLD
WE'RE GONNA LIVE IN
ONE FINE DAY
DREAM ON
SPEND THE NIGHT IN HEAVEN
I'LL BE HERE
TO LIGHT YOUR WAY
SOMEDAY TOMMOROW WILL SMILE
BUT LITTLE GIRL IN THE MEANWHILE
DREAM ON

I WISH YOU COULD HAVE TURNED MY HEAD

*I WISH YOU COULD HAVE TURNED MY HEAD
AND LEFT MY HEART ALONE
EVER SINCE I MET YOU BABY
YOU HAVE DONE ME WRONG
YOU WALKED BY AND YOU SHAKE THAT THING
AND YOU KNOW I'M NOT THAT STRONG
I WISH YOU COULD HAVE TURNED MY HEAD
AND LEFT MY HEART ALONE*

*I WISH YOU COULD HAVE TURNED MY HEAD
AND LEFT MY HEART ALONE
EVER SINCE I MET YOU BABY
YOU HAVE DONE ME WRONG
YOU WALKED BY AND YOU SHAKE THAT THING
AND YOU KNOW I'M NOT THAT STRONG
I WISH YOU COULD HAVE TURNED MY HEAD
AND LEFT MY HEART ALONE*

THE FIRST TIME I LAID EYES ON YOU
GOT CAUGHT UP IN YOUR SWAY
I THOUGHT I DIDN'T HAVE A CHANCE
AND THEN YOU LOOKED MY WAY
FROM THE LONGIN' TO THE LOVIN' GIRL
WE'VE MADE IT ALL THE WAY
BUT FOR ALL THE HUNGER IN MY EYES
MY HEART HAS HAD TO PAY

*I WISH YOU COULD HAVE TURNED MY HEAD
AND LEFT MY HEART ALONE
EVER SINCE I MET YOU BABY
YOU HAVE DONE ME WRONG
YOU WALKED BY AND YOU SHAKE THAT THING
AND YOU KNOW I'M NOT THAT STRONG
I WISH YOU COULD HAVE TURNED MY HEAD
AND LEFT MY HEART ALONE*

(AND LEFT MY HEART ALONE)

by Sonny Throckmorton

I'LL BE TRUE TO YOU

by Alan Rhody

THEY MET UPON A BLUE MOON
THEN THEY PARTED ON A CLOUDY DAY
THEY WERE SO IN LOVE
AND OUT OF SCHOOL
BUT HE WAS GOIN' SO FAR, FAR AWAY
SHE SAID,
I'LL BE TRUE TO YOU
EVEN THOUGH YOU DON'T WANT ME TO
BUT I'LL BE BLUE FOR YOU
EVEN THOUGH YOU'VE ASKED ME NOT TO

WELL THE YEARS DRIFTED BY THEM
AS WE ALL KNOW THEY CAN
HE FOUND OTHER WOMEN
BUT SHE REFUSED OTHER MEN
BUT AS FATE WOULD HAVE IT
THEY MET AGAIN
SHE WAS ON A DOWN-HILL SLIDE
HE WAS JUST SLIDIN' IN

AS HE LOOKED INTO HER EYES THAT NIGHT
HE NEVER REALIZED
THE ONLY REAL LOVE IN HIS LIFE
WAS PASSING BY
WHEN HE TURNED AND LEFT HER THERE
HIS WORDS, "GOODBYE"
HE HEARD HER CALLING OUT TO HIM
AND AS HE WALKED SHE CRIED,
I'VE BEEN TRUE TO YOU
SEEMS LIKE SPEAKIN' TO ME
IS THE LEAST THAT YOU COULD DO
AND I'VE BEEN BLUE FOR YOU
EVEN THOUGH YOU'VE ASKED ME NOT TO

SHE'D BEEN DRINKIN' WAY TOO HARD ONE NIGHT
SHE'D BEEN DRINKIN' WAY TOO LONG
ALONE AND PALE IN A CHEAP HOTEL
SHE DIED THERE IN THE DAWN
KNEELING BY HER GRAVE
OH SO LATE AND OH SO WRONG
HE LONGED TO HOLD HER CLOSE AGAIN
CRYIN' ON AND ON
HE CRIED,
I'LL BE TRUE TO YOU
AFTER ALL THAT I HAVE PUT YOU THROUGH
I'LL BE BLUE FOR YOU
THOUGH YOU NEVER EVEN ASKED ME TO

BEAUTIFUL YOU

by Dave Hanner

PLEASE DON'T CRY
OH, MY
YOU'RE SO BLUE
BUT I'M HERE TO HELP YOU
BEAUTIFUL YOU

YOU NEED SOMEONE
TO GIVE YOU
A LOVE THAT'S TRUE
WELL, I'M HERE TO HELP YOU
BEAUTIFUL YOU

BEAUTIFUL YOU
YOU'LL NEED A MAN SOME DAY
BEAUTIFUL YOU
YOU KNOW I'M HERE TO SAY

DAYS GO BY
OH, MY
WHAT WILL YOU DO
TAKE ME TO HELP YOU
BEAUTIFUL YOU

BEAUTIFUL YOU
I'LL NEVER LET YOU GO
BEAUTIFUL YOU
OUR LOVE WILL ALWAYS GROW

PLEASE DON'T CRY
OH, MY
WHAT WILL YOU DO
TAKE ME TO HELP YOU
BEAUTIFUL YOU

TRYING TO LOVE TWO WOMEN

TRYING TO LOVE TWO WOMEN

by Sonny Throckmorton

TRYING TO LOVE TWO WOMEN
IS LIKE A BALL AND CHAIN
TRYING TO LOVE TWO WOMEN
IS LIKE A BALL AND CHAIN
SOMETIMES THE PLEASURE
AIN'T WORTH THE STRAIN
IT'S A LONG OLD GRIND
AND IT TIRES YOUR MIND

TRYING TO HOLD TWO WOMEN
IS TEARING ME APART
TRYING TO HOLD TWO WOMEN
IS TEARING ME APART
ONE'S GOT MY MONEY
THE OTHER'S GOT MY HEART
IT'S A LONG OLD GRIND
AND IT TIRES YOUR MIND

WHEN YOU TRY TO PLEASE TWO WOMEN
YOU CAN'T PLEASE YOURSELF
WHEN YOU TRY TO PLEASE TWO WOMEN
YOU CAN'T PLEASE YOURSELF
AT BEST IT'S ONLY HALF GOOD
A MAN CAN'T STOCK TWO SHELVES
IT'S A LONG OLD GRIND
AND IT TIRES YOUR MIND

TRYING TO LOVE TWO WOMEN
IS LIKE A BALL AND CHAIN
TRYING TO LOVE TWO WOMEN
IS LIKE A BALL AND CHAIN
SOMETIMES THE PLEASURE
AIN'T WORTH THE STRAIN
IT'S A LONG OLD GRIND
AND IT TIRES YOUR MIND

I GUESS IT NEVER HURTS TO HURT SOMETIMES

by Randy VanWarmer

SOMETIMES I FEEL A WAVE
OF THE PAST BREAK IN MY MIND
AND I KNOW IT'S GONE FOR GOOD
AND IT MAKES ME WANT TO CRY
IS THIS ALL WE GET TO KEEP
AS THE YEARS GO ROLLING BY
JUST THE MEMORY
FOR ALL THE DAYS GONE BY

**OH, YOU'RE ALWAYS IN MY HEART
AND YOU'RE OFTEN ON MY MIND
I WILL NEVER LET IT DIE
JUST AS LONG AS I'M ALIVE
SOMETIMES IT MAKES ME SAD
THAT WE NEVER SAID GOODBYE
WELL I GUESS IT NEVER HURTS
TO HURT SOMETIMES**

YOU TRY TO HOLD ON TO THE MOMENT
BUT TIME WON'T LET YOU STAY
BUT FOR EVERY STEP YOU TAKE
YOU LOSE SOMETHING ON THE WAY
YOU CAN'T LOOK FORWARD TO TOMORROW
AND STILL HOLD ON TO YESTERDAY
OH I HOPE THAT YOU CAN HEAR
WHEN I SAY

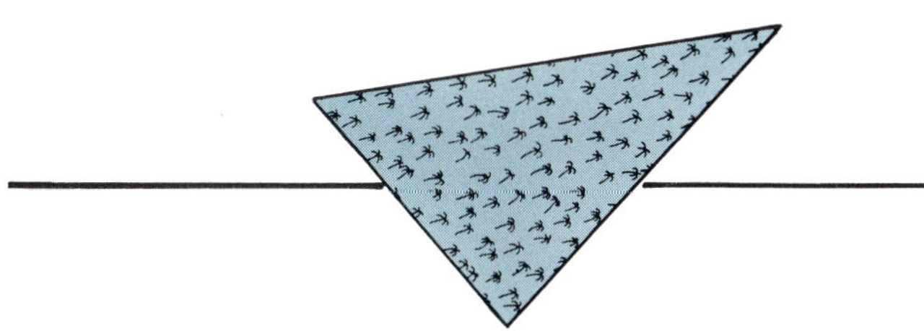

**OH, YOU'RE ALWAYS IN MY HEART
AND YOU'RE OFTEN ON MY MIND
I WILL NEVER LET IT DIE
JUST AS LONG AS I'M ALIVE
SOMETIMES IT MAKES ME SAD
THAT WE NEVER SAID GOODBYE
WELL I GUESS IT NEVER HURTS
TO HURT SOMETIMES**

**NO I GUESS IT NEVER HURTS
TO HURT SOMETIMES**

DOWN

DEEP INSIDE

by Michael Foster and Jimbeau Hinson

I KNOW YOU'RE SCARED, I SEE YOU RUNNIN'
AFRAID OF LOVE, YOU FEEL IT COMIN'
GIRL DON'T MAKE THAT MISTAKE
I'M TELLIN' YOU WHY
WHEN YOU FEEL IT DEEP INSIDE
YOU KNOW IT AIN'T NO LIE

DOWN DEEP INSIDE
LISTEN TO YOUR HEART SPEAK
DOWN DEEP INSIDE
TELLIN' YOU THE TRUTH
DOWN DEEP INSIDE
FEEL THE WAY YOUR HEART BEATS
STIRRIN' UP A FIRE IN YOU
DOWN DEEP INSIDE (DOWN DEEP INSIDE)

SO GIRL HANG ON, YOU CAN TRUST ME
I SWEAR MY LOVE WILL DO YOU JUSTICE
YOU SAY YOUR HEART'S BEEN TORN APART
SO KEEP IT TO YOURSELF
I CAN TELL IT'S BEEN TOO LONG
SINCE YOU LET ANYONE ELSE

DOWN DEEP INSIDE
LISTEN TO YOUR HEART SPEAK
DOWN DEEP INSIDE
TELLIN' YOU THE TRUTH
DOWN DEEP INSIDE
FEEL THE WAY YOUR HEART BEATS
STIRRIN' UP A FIRE IN YOU
DOWN DEEP INSIDE (DOWN DEEP INSIDE)

FANCY FREE

By Jimbeau Hinson & Roy August

I'M SETTIN' FANCY FREE
BECAUSE SHE WANTS TO GO
SHE'S TIRED OF LOVIN' ME
SHE TOLD ME SO
I GUESS SHE DON'T KNOW
JUST HOW MUCH SHE MEANS TO ME
BUT ALONG WITH ALL MY DREAMS
I'M SETTIN' FANCY FREE

YES, I'M SETTIN' FANCY FREE
EVEN THOUGH I LOVE HER STILL
SHE'D BE NO GOOD TO ME
IF I HELD HER AGAINST HER WILL
EVEN THOUGH THAT GIRL
SHE'S THE BEST PART OF MY WORLD
ALONG WITH ALL MY DREAMS
I'M SETTIN' FANCY FREE

OH LORD, YOU JUST DON'T KNOW
HOW IT HURTS TO SAY GOODBYE
SHE DID HER BEST TO STAY
I CAN'T SAY SHE DID NOT TRY
I JUST HOPE THE ROAD
SHE TAKES LEADS BACK TO ME
SO ALONG WITH ALL MY DREAMS
I'M SETTIN' FANCY FREE

YES, I'M SETTIN' FANCY FREE
EVEN THOUGH I LOVE HER STILL
SHE'D BE NO GOOD TO ME
IF I HELD HER AGAINST HER WILL
EVEN THOUGH THAT GIRL
SHE'S THE BEST PART OF MY WORLD
ALONG WITH ALL MY DREAMS
I'M SETTIN' FANCY FREE

THANK GOD FOR KIDS

by Eddy Raven

IF IT WEREN'T FOR KIDS HAVE YOU EVER THOUGHT
THERE WOULDN'T BE NO SANTA CLAUS
OR "LOOK WHAT THE STORK JUST BROUGHT"
THANK GOD FOR KIDS
AND WE'D ALL LIVE IN A QUIET HOUSE
WITHOUT BIG BIRD OR A MICKEY MOUSE
AND KOOL AID ON THE COUCH
THANK GOD FOR KIDS

THANK GOD FOR KIDS
THERE'S MAGIC FOR A WHILE
A SPECIAL KIND OF SUNSHINE IN A SMILE
DO YOU EVER STOP TO THINK OR WONDER WHY
THE NEAREST THING TO HEAVEN
IS A CHILD

"DADDY HOW DOES THIS THING FLY?"
AND A HUNDRED OTHER WHERES AND WHYS
I REALLY DON'T KNOW BUT I TRY
THANK GOD FOR KIDS
WHEN I LOOK DOWN IN THOSE TRUSTING EYES
THAT LOOK TO ME, I REALIZE
THERE'S LOVE THAT I CAN'T BUY
THANK GOD FOR KIDS

THANK GOD FOR KIDS
THERE'S MAGIC FOR A WHILE
A SPECIAL KIND OF SUNSHINE IN A SMILE
DO YOU EVER STOP TO THINK OR WONDER WHY
THE NEAREST THING TO HEAVEN
IS A CHILD

WHEN YOU GET DOWN ON YOUR KNEES TONIGHT
TO THANK THE LORD FOR HIS GUIDING LIGHT
PRAY THEY TURN OUT RIGHT

THANK GOD FOR KIDS

MMM, THANK GOD FOR KIDS

WHEN LOVE CALLS YOU

by Michael Foster

WHEN YOU CROSS MY MIND
I HEAR THE ECHO AND I FEEL THE NIGHT
I HELD YOUR HAND AND SAID
"I'M SO IN LOVE WITH YOU"
BUT YOU DIDN'T LOVE ME TOO

YOU SAID LOVE MAKES YOU SAD
WELL THERE'S SOMETHING YOU SHOULD KNOW
IN THE END
IT'S REALLY ALL YOU'LL HAVE TO SHOW
SO, DON'T TURN AWAY

WHEN LOVE CALLS YOU
SHOW YOUR HEART'S TRUE
OPEN UP AND LET HER IN
THEN THE LESSON WILL BEGIN
SHE'LL UNFOLD YOU
SHE'LL CONTROL YOU
BUT THE TIMES YOU'LL HAVE TO SHOW
ARE THE BEST YOU'LL EVER KNOW
I HOPE LOVE CALLS YOU

WHEN YOU CROSS MY HEART
THERE'S STILL A TENDERNESS I FEEL
IT'S A FEELING THAT I TRIED TO SHARE WITH YOU
BUT YOU DIDN'T WANT TO

NOW SOME WOULD SAY I LOST
BUT KNOWING LOVE WAS WORTH THE COST
AND IF SHE WOULD CALL MY NAME AGAIN TODAY
I'D HAVE TO SAY

WHEN LOVE CALLS YOU
SHOW YOUR HEART'S TRUE
OPEN UP AND LET HER IN
THEN THE LESSON WILL BEGIN
SHE'LL UNFOLD YOU
SHE'LL CONTROL YOU
BUT THE TIMES YOU'LL HAVE TO SHOW
ARE THE BEST YOU'LL EVER KNOW
I HOPE LOVE CALLS YOU

COME ON IN

by Michael Clark

WHEN I GET TIRED AND A LITTLE LONELY
THE WORLD'S TURNED ITS COLD BACK ON ME
WHEN I'M ABOUT TO SWEAR
I AIN'T GOT
A FRIEND LEFT TO MY NAME
INSTEAD OF SINKING A LITTLE LOWER
I START MAKING TRACKS ON OVER
TO A PLACE WHERE THE SUN SHINES DAY AND NIGHT
AND WHERE I KNOW I'LL HEAR YOU SAY

COME ON IN
BABY TAKE YOUR COAT OFF
COME ON IN
BABY TAKE A LOAD OFF
COME ON IN
BABY SHAKE THE BLUES OFF
I'M GONNA LOVE THAT FROWN AWAY
COME ON IN
BABY PUT A SMILE ON
COME ON IN
BABY TELL ME WHAT'S WRONG
COME ON IN
THE BLUES 'LL BE LONG GONE
I'M GONNA LOVE YOUR HURT AWAY

WHEN I FEEL A LONESOME NIGHT COMIN' ON
EVERYTHING I DID ALL DAY WENT WRONG
THERE'S A BLACK CLOUD FOLLOWING ME AROUND
AND I JUST CAN'T GET AWAY
INSTEAD OF SINKING A LITTLE LOWER
I START MAKING TRACKS ON OVER
TO A PLACE WHERE THE SUN SHINES DAY AND NIGHT
AND I KNOW I'LL HEAR YOU SAY

COME ON IN
BABY TAKE YOUR COAT OFF
COME ON IN
BABY TAKE A LOAD OFF
COME ON IN

BABY SHAKE THE BLUES OFF
I'M GONNA LOVE THAT FROWN AWAY
COME ON IN
BABY PUT A SMILE ON
COME ON IN
BABY TELL ME WHAT'S WRONG
COME ON IN
THE BLUES 'LL BE LONG GONE
I'M GONNA LOVE YOUR HURT AWAY

DUANE ALLEN

Duane Allen is a self-avowed songaholic. He is always listening for potential hit songs which The Oak Ridge Boys could record.

He even listens to cassettes tes of submitted material while out mowing the fields on his tractor or while lying on his chiropractor's table. He loves the thrill of discovering a quality, previously unrecorded tune.

He admits to hearing about 100 new songs each week. "I listen to songs pretty much every day of the week," he says. "If you don't make a conscientious effort to find that hit material, somebody else will get it."

Duane has a method and set of standards by which he judges songs. "The first thing I look for is something that just blows me away," he begins. "I find that one song first which becomes the basis for the criteria of how good the others are. So songs eliminate themselves if they don't come up to that quality level."

Ironically some of Duane's favorite songs the group has recorded have never been released as singles, such as "If You Can't Find Love" and "If There Were Only Time For Love."

" 'I Want To Make My Life With You' is my favorite type of song," he explains. "I really like something you can get a lot of emotion and feeling in. That puts it into a ballad category, but I like the fun type songs too, like 'My Radio Sure Sounds Good To Me.' I like songs that make your emotions tingle - that either make you happy and want to clap your hands, or make you cry for joy. I like those kinds of songs best."

While "Elvira" has sold more records than any other Oaks' release, Duane believes that "Thank God For Kids" is *the* song of the group's career thus far. "It is the most important song we ever recorded as far as timing, what it meant to us and how it helped our career," he notes.

Another well timed career song was "I Guess It Never Hurts To Hurt Sometimes." "We had a lot of disc jockeys who said they wanted to hear that Oak Ridge Boys harmony," Duane adds. "On that song we had a nice, gentle harmony with real light voices. We'd never done it that way with Joe singing lead. Although we did it before with me on 'Sail Away.' "

These days Duane has little time to write. He prefers to devote his time and energy to looking for hit songs or to

Don Putnam

working with the group's publishing company, Silverline-Goldline Music, Inc.

Duane never seems to tire of listening to music. "I feel it's a continual process of trying to find the bull's-eye," he reasons. "You're always working your way toward it and you have to be conscious of the fact that the center constantly moves."

Duane Allen and The Oak Ridge Boys are right on target as their hit songs attest. Their marksmenship should keep them at the top of their profession for many years to come.

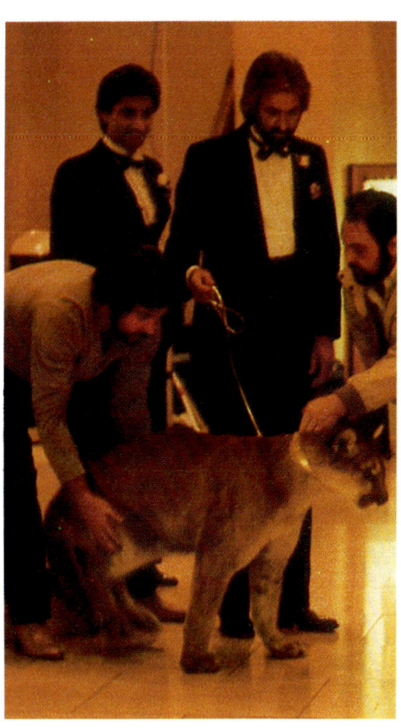

JOE BONSALL

"I'm a fan of The Oak Ridge Boys too!" proclaims Joe Bonsall, the energetic tenor who sings the lead vocals on the group's hits such as "Love Song" and "I Guess It Never Hurts To Hurt Sometimes."

In fact, three of his favorite singers are his partners in song, Duane Allen, William Lee Golden, and Richard Sterban. "I'm just one part of the group, so I can be a fan too," he adds. "Every once in a while I'll get out a whole stack of Oak Ridge Boys albums and play them. When I do listen to them I'm very pleased and very happy with what I hear."

Joe believes that versatility is the key to the Oaks' success. "We've been able to put out so many different kinds of songs with so many different sounds, and at the same time not lose the identity of The Oak Ridge Boys."

"In other words, 'Dream On' doesn't sound like 'Sail Away' which doesn't sound like 'Elvira' which doesn't sound like 'American Made' which doesn't sound like 'Everyday.' and yet, it all is still The Oak Ridge Boys."

With four singers in the group, the Oaks are able to present various lead and harmony vocal combinations. "Our standard sound is Duane on lead, me on top, Golden in the middle and Richard on the bottom," Joe notes. "But we switch around our leads and come up with different sounds. I can sing the lead with Duane above me and Golden underneath me. Richard is always on the bottom. That's a sound like 'Elvira' or 'Love Song.' 'I Guess It Never Hurts To Hurt Sometimes' was me singing the lead with all the other parts stacked underneath. When Golden sings lead we have more of an actual country sound. And when Richard sings lead, well, it's amazing what he can do with his voice. So we can come up with all this diversification of sound within the four of us."

The Oak Ridge Boys have built their career on recording and performing quality songs. "For the most part, I've always thought that every song we've put out as a single I've been happy with," Joe says. " 'Elvira' is one of my favorites because it was such an off the wall thing. 'Bobbie Sue' I've always liked too, mainly because of my love for rock & roll."

" 'Sail Away' was a special song. I remember hearing that on the radio and thinking 'Wow, what a classy record!' When we came on with 'Dream On,' 'Sail Away' and 'Leav-

ing Louisiana In The Broad Daylight' back to back, we established the fact that we could continue to maintain and release a variety of good, commercial music."

The Oak Ridge Boys' audience is as varied as the musical styles the group displays on record and in concert. "Our audience is middle America," Joe says. "It's moms and dads, the kids and the grandparents. That's our audience."

OAK RIDGE BOYS

STEP ON OUT

SPECIAL GUESTS

EXILE AND THE JUDDS

Friday, April 5, 8:00 P.M.

Rupp Arena, Lexington, Kentucky

All Seats Reserved, $13.50 and $12.50

Tickets available at the Rupp Arena Box Office, Both Disc Jockey locations; Radio Shack in Winchester; Record Shop in Richmond; Stereo Warehouse in Pikeville; Soundshop in Somerset; Stacey's in Hazard and Manchester; and WCKQ in Campbellsville; or Charge by Phone 233-3535

Oak Ridge Boys
American Made
OAK RIDGE BOYS
'85
OAK RIDGE BOYS
STEP ON OUT
ALL ACCESS
ADMIT ONE ADULT
IF STUB ATTACHED
$13.50
THE OA
ADULT $13

Don Putnam

WILLIAM LEE GOLDEN

For William Lee Golden "Thank God For Kids" will always be a magical song. The gentle-minded, soft-spoken baritone sang the lead vocal on this Eddy Raven-penned classic which was included on the Oaks' 1982 album - "Oak Ridge Boys—Christmas."

Both the album and single were the 13th Christmas recording to be certified gold by the Recording Industry Association of America (R.I.A.A.) in the organization's history.

"We listened to the song during some of our screening sessions," Golden recalls. "I was chosen to sing the lead on it somehow. It's the only song I sang lead in on the album."

The Oaks recorded "Thank God For Kids" during the spring of 1982. "It was the song that actually got the whole ball rolling for a Christmas album." Golden notes. "It was kind of like planting a seed and cultivating it until harvest time."

The song has become somewhat of an unofficial anthem for the group's ongoing campaign for the prevention of child abuse. In the past the Oaks have sponsored the "Stars for Children Concert" to raise funds for the cause. "It's a song that we can sing all year long, and not just during the holi-

day season," Golden adds.

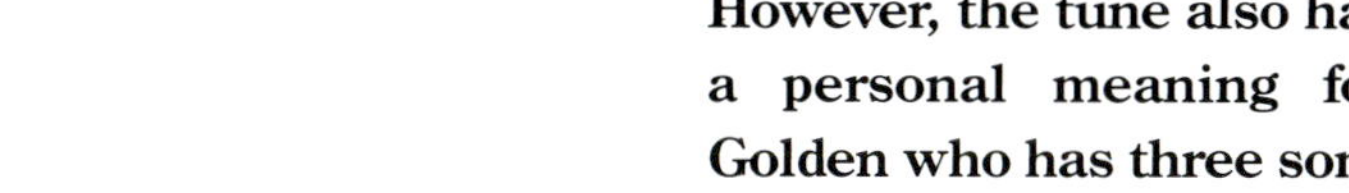

However, the tune also has a personal meaning for Golden who has three sons of his own. His grandson was born on December 19, 1982 during the time that "Thank God for Kids" was so popular. "With the record becoming such a tremendous radio hit and then my becoming a grandfather, the song took on a completely different meaning than it did when we first recorded it," he explains.

"Thank God For Kids" also has had a profound impact on the Oaks' audience. "The first time we ever did it in concert was in Pine Bluff, Arkansas at a taping of an HBO special," Golden says. "It got a tremendous reaction. It was one of those unexpected ovations at the conclusion of the song. I think that it had a much stronger impact than we had originally expected it to have."

Golden is decidedly the most country-sounding vocalist of the four singers. "I don't deny that," Golden attests. "I grew up in the rural south, so I know what that's about. You absorb all that—the moods and the feeling; it becomes a part of you."

One song Golden can relate to is "Ozark Mountain Jubilee,"

which he interprets with lyrical eloquence. "I loved that song from the beginning," he says. "I enjoy singing it every night."

While Golden is a marvelous interpreter of lyric and melody, he admits he has never written a song. "I've never been able to write," he adds. "My mother writes poetry and my sons write music. It's a special talent that I respect."

Songs are the heart of the Oak's success. "We've been fortunate, and I'm real thankful for that," Golden concludes. "It's all in the songs. If it wasn't for the writers it wouldn't be nearly as easy for us to do what we enjoy doing so much."

No doubt songwriters are mighty thankful for vocalists like William Lee Golden and the other Oaks who sing life into their words and melodies.

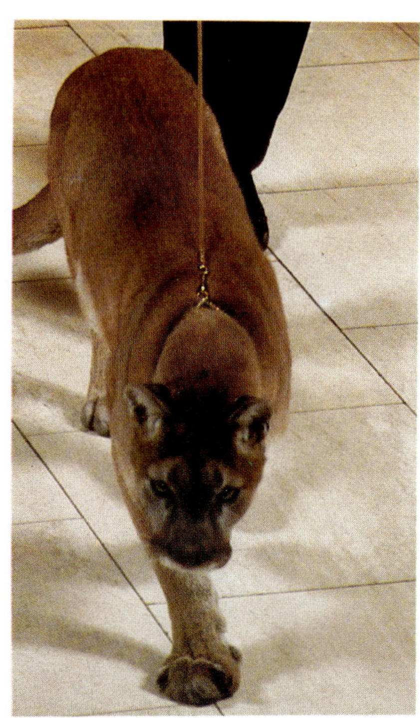

RICHARD STERBAN

Of all the songs The Oak Ridge Boys have recorded, none is more closely identified with them than the double platinum selling single, "Elvira." Richard Sterban knew it was a hit song the first time the group performed it on stage when he walked up to the microphone and sang in his inimitable deep voice, "oom pah pah mau mau." That vintage Sterban vocal part became instantly identifiable and has often been imitated but never duplicated.

"We were in Seattle," he recalls. "We rehearsed it that afternoon and added it to our show that night. The response was unbelievable. We had to repeat the song five times in the show. People would not let us quit doing the song. It got a bigger response than all our previous hits which we sang that night. I looked at the guys and said, 'Fellas, I think this is the song we've been looking for.' "

Of course, the Oaks has no idea that "Elvira" would become one of the biggest hit records in the music industry's recent memory. "I still wonder what it was about that song that made it so big," Richard muses. "It's really hard to put your finger on. There are so many things involved—the timing was right, the novel bass part hooked people, and the music tracks were so strong—everything just fell

into place at the right time. More so than any other record we've ever cut, the excitement was in the grooves. That song just sounds like a hit."

Although Richard rarely sings the lead vocal parts, his voice which can literally rattle the rafters, is an integral part of The Oak Ridge Boys' sound. He says, "A good song for a low voice is more difficult to find. A lot of the time the way I am heard is not so much on the lead but by sticking in a lick here and there like 'Elvira' or 'Ba Ba Bobbie Sue.' "

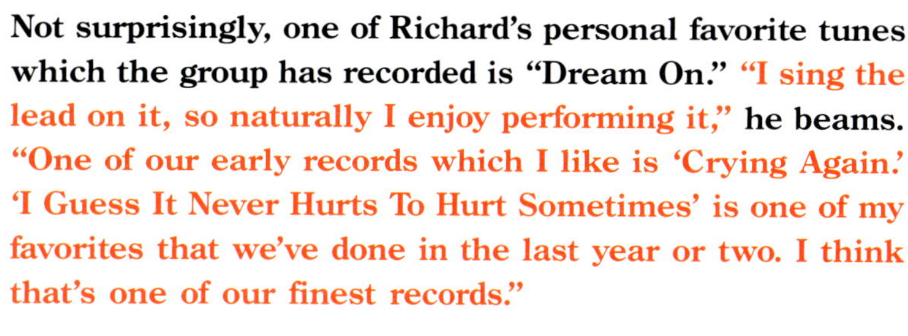

Not surprisingly, one of Richard's personal favorite tunes which the group has recorded is "Dream On." "I sing the lead on it, so naturally I enjoy performing it," he beams. "One of our early records which I like is 'Crying Again.' 'I Guess It Never Hurts To Hurt Sometimes' is one of my favorites that we've done in the last year or two. I think that's one of our finest records."

Richard believes that the primary reason The Oak Ridge Boys have achieved such immense popularity, and have been able to maintain that level of success, is that the group builds its career upon the music it records.

"Over the years the real reward has been that people are still coming out by the thousands to our concerts, and every album we put out goes Gold," he adds. "That's the true test of whether or not the public likes your music."

Judging by their success, Richard Sterban and his singing partners are providing their fans with precisely the kind of music they want to hear.

SAIL AWAY

by Rafe VanHoy

ACROSS THE BAY A LADY WAITS
TO HOLD ME TIGHT
AND MY BOAT AND I ARE READY TO SET SAIL
IF THE WEATHER KEEPS ON HOLDIN'
AND THE WIND IS RIGHT
I'LL BE WRAPPED UP IN MY SWEET ONE'S ARMS TONIGHT

AND WE WILL SAIL AWAY
ON THE WINGS OF LOVE INTO THE NIGHT
CAST OUT OUR FORTUNES ON THE SEA
THEN WE WILL GO TO SLEEP TOGETHER
WITH THE ROCKING OF THE WATER
AND DREAM OF HOW OUR LIFE WILL SOMEDAY BE
WHEN SHE SAILS AWAY WITH ME

AS I SKIP ACROSS THE WAVES
MY SAILS ARE HIGH AND FULL
MY MIND IS ON THE ONE I WAIT TO SEE
AND I DREAM ABOUT AN ISLAND SOMEWHERE IN MY MIND
WHERE SOMEDAY I WILL TAKE HER OFF WITH ME

AND WE WILL SAIL AWAY
ON THE WINGS OF LOVE INTO THE NIGHT
CAST OUT OUR FORTUNES ON THE SEA
THEN WE WILL GO TO SLEEP TOGETHER
WITH THE ROCKING OF THE WATER
AND DREAM OF HOW OUR LIFE WILL SOMEDAY BE
WHEN SHE SAILS AWAY WITH ME

THEN A SMILE COMES UPON ME
AS I LOOK ACROSS THE BOW
I SEE A LADY ON THE SIDE
BUT SHE WILL WAIT NO MORE
AS I HEAD FOR THE SHORE
'CAUSE TONIGHT I'M GONNA TAKE HER FOR A RIDE

AND WE WILL SAIL AWAY
ON THE WINGS OF LOVE INTO THE NIGHT
CAST OUT OUR FORTUNES ON THE SEA
THEN WE WILL GO TO SLEEP TOGETHER
WITH THE ROCKING OF THE WATER
AND DREAM OF HOW OUR LIFE WILL SOMEDAY BE
WHEN SHE SAILS AWAY WITH ME

ELVIRA

by Dallas Frazier

ELVIRA
ELVIRA
MY HEART'S ON FIRE
FOR ELVIRA

EYES THAT LOOK LIKE HEAVEN
LIPS LIKE CHERRY WINE
THAT GIRL CAN SHO' NUFF MAKE MY LITTLE LIGHT SHINE
I GET A FUNNY FEELING
UP AND DOWN MY SPINE
'CAUSE I KNOW THAT MY ELVIRA'S MINE
I'M SINGIN'

ELVIRA
ELVIRA
MY HEART'S ON FIRE
FOR ELVIRA

GIDDY-UP
A OOM PAH PAH OOM PAH PAH MAU MAU
GIDDY-UP A OOM PAH PAH OOM PAH PAH MAU MAU
HI YO SILVER AWAY

TONIGHT I'M GONNA MEET HER
AT THE HUNGRY HOUSE CAFE
AND I'M GONNA GIVE HER ALL THE LOVE I CAN, YES I AM
SHE'S GONNA JUMP AND HOLLER
'CAUSE I SAVED UP MY LAST TWO DOLLAR
AND WE'RE GONNA SEARCH AND FIND THAT PREACHER MAN

ELVIRA
ELVIRA
MY HEART'S ON FIRE
FOR ELVIRA

GIDDY-UP
A OOM PAH PAH OOM PAH PAH MAU MAU
GIDDY-UP A OOM PAH PAH OOM PAH PAH MAU MAU
HI YO SILVER AWAY

ELVIRA
ELVIRA
MY HEART'S ON FIRE
FOR ELVIRA

HEART OF MINE

by Michael Foster

THERE WASN'T MUCH LOVE ON THE DAY YOU CAME
I WAS FEELING MY WAY WITH A HEART GONE LAME
LIFE WAS SO COLD RIGHT THEN
I THOUGHT I'D NEVER LOVE AGAIN
ALL MY DREAMS OF ROMANCE
FLEW AWAY WITH THE WIND
OH
MY HEART BEATS SLOW

HEART OF MINE
CAN WE TRY IT ONE MORE TIME
CAN YOU HELP BUT LOVE A GIRL SO FREE SO KIND
LONELY TEARS
KEPT ME WAITING ALL THESE YEARS
FOR THE DAY I FELT THE JOY OF LOVE INSIDE
WHEN MY HEART'S ALIVE

BELIEVE ME I KNOW THAT THE TRUTH SOUNDS STRANGE (OH YEAH)
HOW AN INNOCENT SMILE MADE MY WHOLE LIFE CHANGE (UH HUH)
YOU CALL IT COINCIDENCE
BUT I KNOW SHE WAS HEAVEN SENT
WHEN I FELT THAT MY HEART
WAS BEGINNING TO MEND
NOW
MY HEART BEATS FAST

HEART OF MINE
I THINK WE MADE IT JUST IN TIME
WE CAN'T HELP BUT LOVE A GIRL SO FREE SO KIND
LONELY TEARS
KEPT ME LOOKING ALL THOSE YEARS
AND TODAY I FELT THE JOY OF LOVE INSIDE
YES MY HEART'S ALIVE
AND GROWING STRONGER ALL THE TIME

TOUCH A HAND,

MAKE A FRIEND

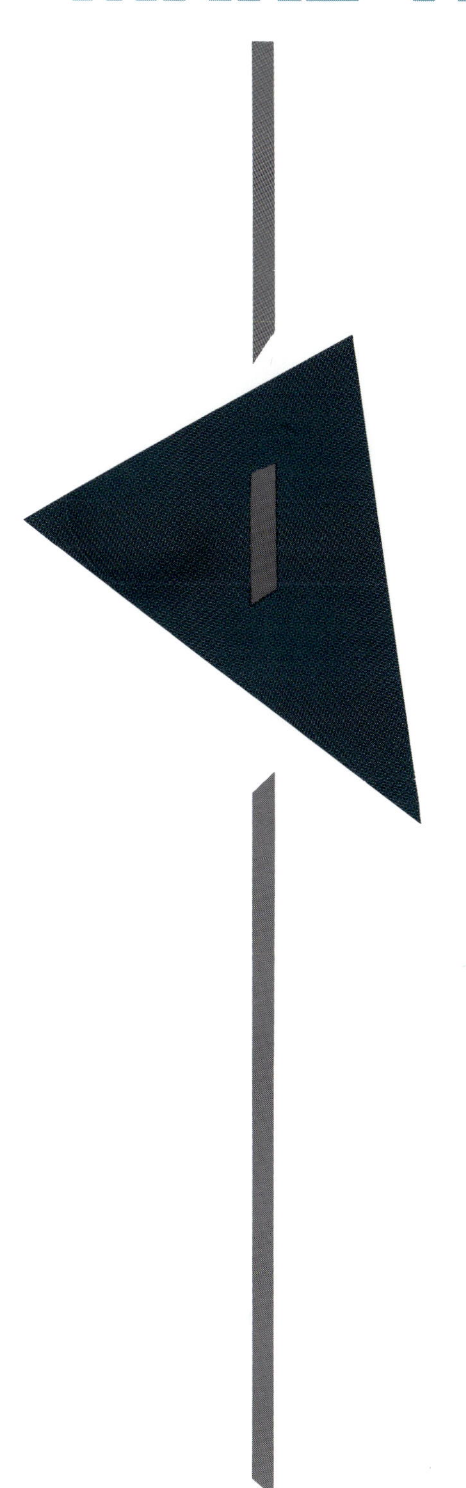

by Homer Banks, Raymond Jackson, & Carl Hampton

CAN'T YOU FEEL IT IN YOUR BONES
A CHANGE IS COMIN' ON
FROM EVERY WALK OF LIFE
PEOPLE SEEIN' THE LIGHT

CAN'T YOU FEEL IT IN YOUR HEART NOW
A NEW THING IS TAKIN' SHAPE
REACH OUT AND TOUCH A HAND
MAKE A FRIEND IF YOU CAN

REACH OUT AND TOUCH A HAND
MAKE A FRIEND IF YOU CAN
REACH OUT AND TOUCH A HAND
MAKE A FRIEND IF YOU CAN

I'VE READ ABOUT YOU MY FRIEND
AIN'T IT TIME TO COME ON IN
WE CAN FIND A BETTER WAY
WHY DON'T YOU JOIN US TODAY

CAN'T YOU FEEL IT IN YOUR HEART NOW
A NEW THING IS TAKIN' SHAPE
REACH OUT AND TOUCH A HAND
MAKE A FRIEND IF YOU CAN

REACH OUT AND TOUCH A HAND
MAKE A FRIEND IF YOU CAN
REACH OUT AND TOUCH A HAND
MAKE A FRIEND IF YOU CAN

IT'S BEEN REFLECTED IN THE ATTITUDES
OF OTHER PEOPLE JUST LIKE YOU
REACH OUT AND TOUCH A HAND
MAKE A FRIEND IF YOU CAN

CAN'T YOU FEEL IT IN YOUR HEART NOW
A NEW THING IS TAKING SHAPE
REACH OUT AND TOUCH A HAND
MAKE A FRIEND IF YOU CAN

REACH OUT AND TOUCH A HAND
MAKE A FRIEND IF YOU CAN
REACH OUT AND TOUCH A HAND
MAKE A FRIEND IF YOU CAN

WHEN I'M WITH YOU

by Mitch Humphries & Jerry Michael

I KNOW IT'S LATE TO BE CALLING
BUT I JUST CAN'T GET TO SLEEP
I'VE GOT SOMETHING HEAVY ON MY MIND
AND I'M AFRAID IT JUST WON'T KEEP

YOU ALWAYS UNDERSTAND MY FEELINGS
AND YOU LOVE THE HURT AWAY
THERE'S NOT A SINGLE DOUBT LEFT IN MY MIND
WITH YOU IS WHERE I NEED TO STAY

WHEN I'M WITH YOU
I FIND MYSELF BELIEVING IN YOUR LOVE
JUST ENOUGH
TO MAKE MY DREAM COME TRUE
WHEN I'M WITH YOU
I WONDER WHERE DREAMS STOP AND YOU BEGIN
TIME AND AGAIN
THE DREAM COMES TRUE FOR ME WHEN I'M WITH YOU

MY CUP IS FULL AND RUNNING OVER
WITH SWEET LOVE THAT CAME FROM YOU
WHAT I'M SAYING'S COMING FROM MY HEART
I'LL BE FOREVER LOVING YOU

WHEN I'M WITH YOU
I FIND MYSELF BELIEVING IN YOUR LOVE
JUST ENOUGH
TO MAKE MY DREAM COME TRUE
WHEN I'M WITH YOU
I WONDER WHERE DREAMS STOP AND YOU BEGIN
TIME AND AGAIN
THE DREAM COMES TRUE FOR ME WHEN I'M WITH YOU
THE DREAM COMES TRUE FOR ME WHEN I'M WITH YOU

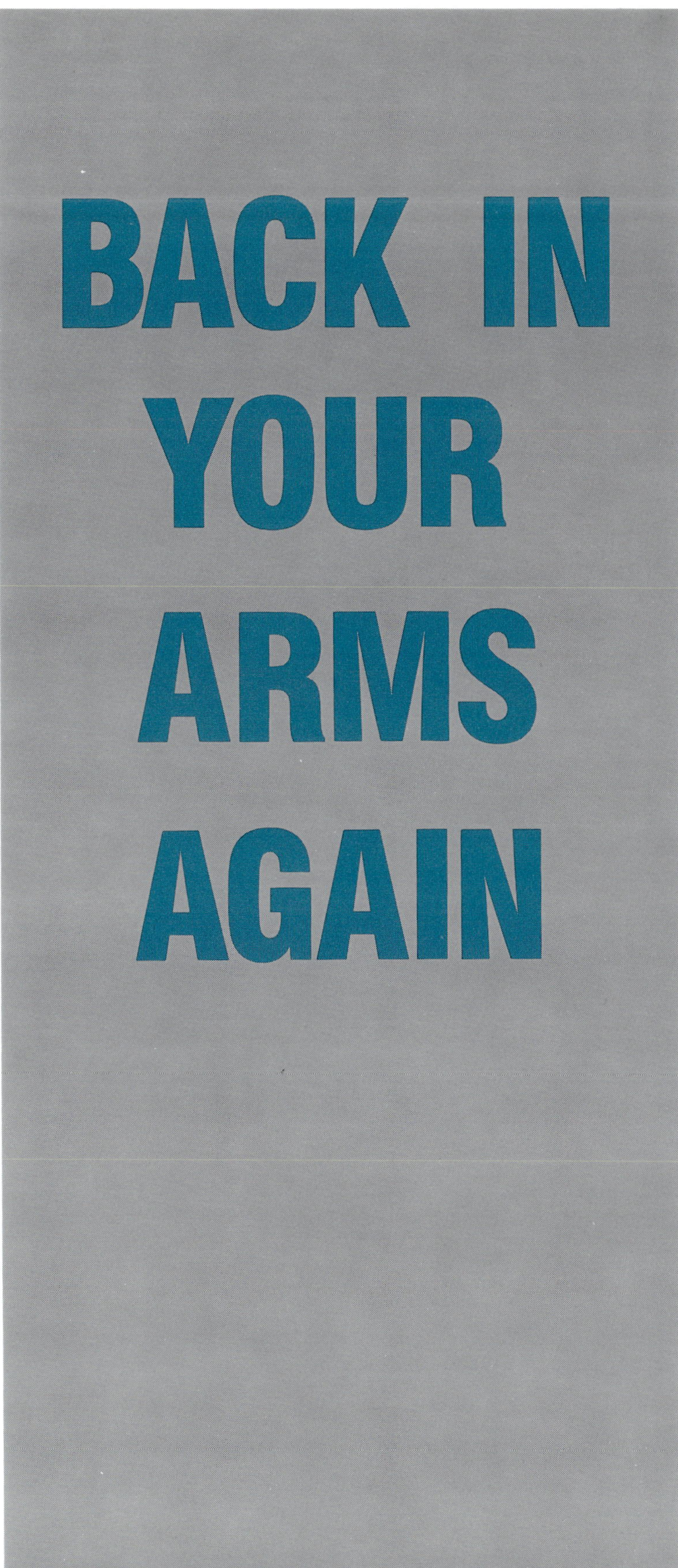

by Rusty Golden

THE CALL THAT I MADE TONIGHT
WAS SUCH A LONG TIME DUE
BABY HOW LONG SINCE I'VE HEARD FROM YOU
I DON'T REALLY KNOW WHAT'S HAPPENING HERE TO ME
ALL THAT I KNOW IS THAT I LONG TO BE

BACK IN YOUR ARMS AGAIN
I NEED YOUR LOVE
ALL I CAN GET
WHATEVER IT TAKES
YOU KNOW I'LL BE THERE
BACK IN YOUR ARMS
BACK IN YOUR ARMS

THE LAST TIME I SPOKE TO YOU
YOU TOLD ME THAT WE WERE THROUGH
THAT YOU HAD FOUND THAT SPECIAL SOMEONE NEW
NOW THAT I REALLY KNOW
THIS FEELING OF BEING FREE
I HOPE THAT YOU KNOW WHERE I LONG TO BE

BACK IN YOUR ARMS AGAIN
I NEED YOUR LOVE
ALL I CAN GET
WHATEVER IT TAKES
YOU KNOW I'LL BE THERE
BACK IN YOUR ARMS
BACK IN YOUR ARMS

Don Putnam

AIN'T NO CURE FOR THE ROCK AND ROLL

by Walter Carter

I WAS STILL A BOY WHEN IT HAPPENED TO ME
I STARTED SHAKING UNCONTROLLABLY
DOCTOR CAME AND HE SHOOK HIS HEAD
AND MAMA CRIED WHEN THE DOCTOR SAID

YOU CAN SEE THE LOOK ON THE POOR BOY'S FACE
WELL HE'S BEEN TOOK WITH A TERMINAL CASE
AIN'T A PRAYER, NO THERE AIN'T NO HOPE
YOU CAN HEAR THE BEAT ON MY STETHOSCOPE

OH, WELL IT'S ROCK AND ROLL, ROCK AND ROLL
CAN'T BE STOPPED
OUT OF CONTROL
IT'S GOT HIS BODY
NOW IT'S AFTER HIS SOUL
AIN'T NO CURE FOR THE ROCK AND ROLL

IT WASN'T VERY LONG UNTIL THE DREAD DISEASE
SPREAD THROUGH THE VERY BEST FAMILIES
FOLKS HAD HEARD ABOUT THE DEVIL'S CURSE
BUT THEY ALL AGREED THIS WAS A WHOLE LOT WORSE

THE TRAGEDY OF MY NEIGHBORHOOD
WAS MY BEST FRIEND, JOHNNY B. GOODE
AND BOTH OUR GIRLFRIENDS CAUGHT IT TOO
I'M TALKING ABOUT ELVIRA AND MY BOBBIE SUE

OH, WELL IT'S ROCK AND ROLL, ROCK AND ROLL
CAN'T BE STOPPED
OUT OF CONTROL
IT'S GOT HIS BODY
NOW IT'S AFTER HIS SOUL
AIN'T NO CURE FOR THE ROCK AND ROLL

OH, WALKING THE STREET WITH A FRIEND OF MINE
SHUFFLING MY FEET, JUST A KEEPING TIME
FROM OUT OF NOWHERE CAME A GUITAR LICK
NOTHING FANCY BUT IT DID THE TRICK

WELL, I TURNED INTO A LITTLE DANCING FOOL
I THANK MY FRIEND FOR KEEPING HIS COOL
HE SAID, GIVE HIM ROOM AND HE'LL BE JUST FINE
HE'S BEEN THIS WAY SINCE NINETEEN FIFTY-NINE

OH, WELL IT'S ROCK AND ROLL, ROCK AND ROLL
CAN'T BE STOPPED
OUT OF CONTROL
IT'S GOT HIS BODY
NOW IT'S AFTER HIS SOUL
AIN'T NO CURE FOR THE ROCK AND ROLL

WOULD THEY LOVE HIM DOWN IN SHREVEPORT

by Bobby Braddock

IF THEY SAW HIM RIDING IN
LONG HAIR FLYING IN THE WIND
WOULD THEY LOVE HIM DOWN IN SHREVEPORT TODAY?
IF THEY HEARD HE WAS A JEW
AND A PALESTINEAN TOO
WOULD THEY LOVE HIM DOWN IN NASHVILLE TODAY?

IF THEY SAW HIM TALK WITH EASE
TO THE JUNKIES, WHORES AND THIEVES
WOULD THE LOVE HIM OUT IN WICHITA TODAY?
WOULD THE RICH MEN THINK IT FUNNY
IF HE SAID GIVE UP YOUR MONEY
WOULD THEY LOVE HIM UP ON WALL STREET TODAY?

IF HE MADE THE WINE FROM WATER
GAVE IT TO THEIR SONS AND DAUGHTERS
WHAT WOULD THE FOLKS IN SALT LAKE CITY SAY?
IF HE TALKED OF BROTHERHOOD
AS HE WALKED THEIR NEIGHBORHOODS
WOULD THEY LOVE HIM UP IN BOSTON TODAY?

IF HE SAID, "LOVE THOSE WHO USE YOU,
AND FORGIVE THOSE WHO ABUSE YOU"
IF HE TURNED THE OTHER CHEEK
WHAT WOULD YOU SAY?
WOULD YOU LAUGH AND CALL HIM CRAZY
AND JUST SEND HIM ON HIS WAY
IF JESUS CAME TO YOUR TOWN TODAY

CRYIN' AGAIN

by Rafe VanHoy & Don Cook

YOU TOLD ME THAT OUR LOVE WAS FOREVER
BUT YOU NEVER REALLY MEANT IT THAT WAY
YOU SAID WE HAD A SWEET SITUATION
BUT I'M WAKING UP WITHOUT YOU TODAY

CRYIN' AGAIN
WE'RE OUT OF LOVE AGAIN
CRYIN' AGAIN
LIKE WE'VE NEARLY ALWAYS BEEN
CRYIN' AGAIN
I WONDER WHEN I WON'T BE
CRYIN' AGAIN

I THOUGHT WE HAD A REAL UNDERSTANDING
BUT YOU NEVER UNDERSTOOD WHAT I SAID
THE MAGIC DIDN'T LAST LIKE WE PLANNED IT
BUT WE'VE WASTED ALL THE FEELINGS INSTEAD

CRYIN' AGAIN
WE'RE OUT OF LOVE AGAIN
CRYIN' AGAIN
LIKE WE'VE NEARLY ALWAYS BEEN
CRYIN' AGAIN
I WONDER WHEN I WON'T BE
CRYIN' AGAIN

Y'ALL COME BACK SALOON

by Sharon Vaughn

SHE PLAYED TAMBOURINE
WITH A SILVER JINGLE
AND SHE MUST HAVE KNOWN THE WORDS TO AT LEAST A MILLION TUNES
BUT THE ONE MOST REQUESTED
BY THE MAN SHE KNEW AS "COWBOY"
WAS THE LATE NIGHT BENEDICTION
AT THE Y'ALL COME BACK SALOON

IN A VOICE SOFT AND TREMBLING
SHE'D SING HER SONG TO COWBOY
AS A SMOKEY HALO CIRCLED 'ROUND HER RAVEN HAIR
AND ALL THE FALLEN ANGELS
THE PINBALL PLAYIN' ROUNDERS
STOPPED THE GAMES THAT THEY'D BEEN PLAYIN'
FOR THE LOSERS' EVENING PRAYER

FADED LOVE AND FADED MEM'RIES
HOW THEY LINGER IN A MIND
MILES AND YEARS PLAYED THE COWBOY
LIKE AN OLD MELODY
OUT OF TUNE AND OUT OF TIME

EV'RY NIGHT IN THE SHADOWS
THINKING BACK ON AMARILLO
HE'D DREAM OF BETTER DAYS AND ASK FOR FADED LOVE
LIFTING HIGH HIS GLASS IN HONOR
OF THE LADY AND HER SONG
HE PAID HIS CHECK THEN LONELY
WALKED THAT BROKEN COWBOY HOME

SHE PLAYED TAMBOURINE
WITH A SILVER JINGLE
AND SHE MUST HAVE KNOWN THE WORDS TO AT LEAST A MILLION TUNES
BUT THE ONE MOST REQUESTED
BY THE MAN SHE KNEW AS "COWBOY"
WAS THE LATE NIGHT BENEDICTION
AT THE Y'ALL COME BACK SALOON

HEART ON THE LINE (OPERATOR, OPERATOR)

by Larry Willoughby & Janet Willoughby

I'VE THOUGHT IT OVER HOW IT'S COME TO THIS
I MUST HAVE LOST ALL MY COMMON SENSE
I BEEN CHASIN' A DREAM
RUNNIN' THROUGH MY MIND
I CALLED HER UP TO SAY HOW I FELT
BUT JUST BEFORE I COULD GET IT OUT
SHE WAS GONE
THE SILENCE WAS ON THE LINE
I DIDN'T HEAR A WORD
SHE JUST HUNG UP THE TELEPHONE

OPERATOR, OPERATOR
WOULD YOU BE SO KIND
AS TO RECONNECT MY NUMBER
I JUST SPENT MY LAST DIME (MY LAST DIME)
SHE'S PUT MY LOVE ON HOLD
AND MY HEART IS ON THE LINE

WELL I WAS ALWAYS JUST ONE STEP AHEAD
YET CLOSE ENOUGH TO KEEP MY FINGERS WET
I'VE BEEN ACTING TO FOOL NO ONE BUT MYSELF, YES I HAVE

WELL, I'M WILLING TO TALK
IF YOU'RE WILLING TO HEAR
THE CHOICE OF WORDS IS MY BIGGEST FEAR
I'D SAY ANYTHING
JUST TO CHANGE YOUR MIND
YOU'VE GOT MY LOVE ON HOLD
AND MY HEART IS ON THE LINE

OH, OPERATOR, OPERATOR
WOULD YOU BE SO KIND
AS TO RECONNECT MY NUMBER
I JUST SPENT MY LAST DIME (MY LAST DIME)
SHE'S PUT MY LOVE ON HOLD
AND MY HEART IS ON THE LINE

MAKE MY LIFE WITH YOU

by Gary Burr

HERE IN THE DAY
HERE IN THE LIGHT
ALL I CAN SEE IS YOU LAST NIGHT
LIT BY THE MOON
STILL BY MY SIDE
LOVING ARMS OPEN WIDE

AND THE LOVE THAT COMES OVER ME
IS ENOUGH TO MAKE ME STAY
IS IT LIFE LIVED SEP'RATELY
IS LIFE ALL IT OUGHT TO BE
OH IF IT WERE UP TO ME
I'D MAKE MY LIFE WITH YOU

SOME PEOPLE SAY
IT'S A DANGEROUS GAME
I'LL TAKE MY CHANCES JUST THE SAME
IF LOVE IS A GAME
AND YOU ARE THE PRIZE
YOU STANDING HERE IS NO SURPRISE

AND THE LOVE THAT COMES OVER ME
IS ENOUGH TO MAKE ME STAY
IS IT LIFE LIVED SEP'RATELY
IS LIFE ALL IT OUGHT TO BE
OH IF IT WERE UP TO ME
I'D MAKE MY LIFE WITH YOU

IS IT LIFE LIVED SEP'RATELY
IS LIFE ALL IT OUGHT TO BE
OH IF IT WERE UP TO ME
I'D MAKE MY LIFE WITH YOU

YOU'RE THE ONE

by Bob Morrison

MANY'S THE TIME
I HAVE LOOKED IN THE WATER
AND HAD NO REFLECTION TO SHOW
OH, AND MANY'S THE TIME
I HAVE STOOD AT THE CROSSROADS
NOT KNOWING WHICH WAY TO GO

MANY'S THE TIME
SOMEONE LAY CLOSE BESIDE ME
AND I DON'T REMEMBER HER NAME
THEY'LL SAY THAT I'M
JUST A SMILE AND A MOMENT
BUT THAT WAS BEFORE YOU CAME

*YOU'RE THE ONE IN A MILLION
YOU'RE THE ONE, YOU'RE THE ONE
YOU'RE THE ONE IN A MILLION I SEE
YOU'RE THE ONE IN A MILLION
YOU'RE THE ONE, YOU'RE THE ONE
YOU'RE THE ONE IN A MILLION FOR ME*

NOW ALL OF THE OTHERS
WERE PLACES TO GO TO
WHEN I HAD NO WHERE TO SLEEP
WELL, I NEVER MADE
ANY PROMISES TO THEM
NONE THEY'D EXPECT ME TO KEEP

*YOU'RE THE ONE IN A MILLION
YOU'RE THE ONE, YOU'RE THE ONE
YOU'RE THE ONE IN A MILLION I SEE
YOU'RE THE ONE IN A MILLION
YOU'RE THE ONE, YOU'RE THE ONE
YOU'RE THE ONE IN A MILLION FOR ME*

*WELL, YOU'RE THE ONE IN A MILLION
YOU'RE THE ONE, YOU'RE THE ONE
YOU'RE THE ONE IN A MILLION I SEE
YOU'RE THE ONE IN A MILLION
YOU'RE THE ONE, YOU'RE THE ONE
YOU'RE THE ONE IN A MILLION FOR ME*

HOW LONG HAS IT BEEN

by Michael Foster & Marshall Morgan

HEY MY OLD LOVER AND FRIEND
HOW LONG HAS IT BEEN
SINCE WE LAY TOGETHER
YOU KNOW HOW I'D LOVE TO SEE YOU AGAIN
HOW LONG HAS IT BEEN

ANOTHER SUN SETS
AND THOUGH YOU'RE FAR AWAY
IT'S HARD TO FORGET
THE GOOD DAYS WE SPENT
I CAN'T HELP MY SELF
WHEN FROM TIME TO TIME
THE MEMORIES SWELL
THERE'S NO ONE TO TELL

NOW I KNOW
THE CHANCES ARE WE GAVE IT UP TOO SOON
WHEN MORNING TURNED TO AFTERNOON
AND SOON THE SUN HAD SET
THE GOOD TIMES SLIPPED AWAY
SO I THOUGHT I'D CALL JUST TO SAY

MY OLD LOVER AND FRIEND
HOW LONG HAS IT BEEN
SINCE WE LAY TOGETHER
YOU KNOW HOW I'D LOVE TO SEE YOU AGAIN
HOW LONG HAS IT BEEN

DAYS ARE SHORT NIGHTS ARE LONG
MY DREAMS ARE ALL THE SAME
TAKE ME BACK TO THE DAYS WHEN WE WERE YOUNG
TAKE ME BACK

NOW I KNOW
THE CHANCES ARE WE GAVE IT UP TOO SOON
WHEN MORNING TURNED TO AFTERNOON
AND SOON THE SUN HAD SET
THE GOOD TIMES SLIPPED AWAY
SO I THOUGHT I'D CALL JUST TO SAY

MY OLD LOVER AND FRIEND
HOW LONG HAS IT BEEN
SINCE WE LAY TOGETHER
YOU KNOW HOW I'D LOVE TO SEE YOU AGAIN
I MISS YOU, I MISS YOU, I MISS YOU
HOW LONG HAS IT BEEN

ONLY ONE I LOVE

by Michael Foster & Jimbeau Hinson

MORNING EYES CALLIN'
LIKE THE SUN RISIN'
YOUR SMILE COMES SHININ' THROUGH
LOVERS HEARTS WAKIN'
DREAMY LOVE MAKIN'
ONCE AGAIN I WANT TO TELL YOU BABY

YOU'RE THE ONLY ONE
ONLY ONE I LOVE
YOU'RE THE ONLY ONE
THAT MAKES ME WANT TO
PUSH THE WORLD AWAY
HOLD YOU CLOSE AND SAY
YOU'RE THE ONLY ONE I LOVE

EVENING EYES GREET ME
LOVIN' HANDS GENTLY
MAKE MY WORRIES DISAPPEAR
RUB MY TIRED SHOULDERS
TALK THE DAY OVER
'CAUSE THE ONLY ONE THAT CARES IS YOU GIRL

YOU'RE THE ONLY ONE
ONLY ONE I LOVE
YOU'RE THE ONLY ONE
THAT MAKES ME WANT TO
PUSH THE WORLD AWAY
HOLD YOU CLOSE AND SAY
YOU'RE THE ONLY ONE I LOVE

WHEN YOU GET TO THE HEART

by Tony Brown, Norro Wilson, & Wayland Holyfield

GIRL COME SIT BESIDE ME
YOU KNOW HOW YOU EXCITE ME
TONIGHT LET'S LOCK THE WORLD OUTSIDE OUR DOOR
SOMETIMES IT GETS SO CRAZY
AND LORD KNOWS IT'S NOT EASY
TO FIND THE TIME TO LOVE ANYMORE
THE THINGS THAT WE GO AFTER
THEY REALLY JUST DON'T MATTER
IT'S NOT THE WAY WE STARTED OUT
ALL WE HAD WAS EACH OTHER
AND BABE, THAT'S WHAT IT'S ALL ABOUT

WHEN YOU BREAK IT ALL DOWN
AND YOU STRIP IT APART
THERE'S JUST ONE THING THAT MATTERS AT ALL
WHEN YOU GET TO THE HEART
WHEN THE SMOKE CLEARS AWAY
AND WE SEE WHERE WE ARE
WE'LL SEE ALL THAT REALLY MATTERS IS LOVE
WHEN YOU GET TO THE HEART

SO BABY LET'S GET DOWN TO IT
ALL WE GOT TO DO IS DO IT
YOU KNOW THAT WE CAN WORK IT OUT
ALL WE'VE GOT IS EACH OTHER
AND BABE THAT'S WHAT IT'S ALL ABOUT

WHEN YOU BREAK IT ALL DOWN
AND YOU STRIP IT APART
THERE'S JUST ONE THING THAT MATTERS AT ALL
WHEN YOU GET TO THE HEART
WHEN THE SMOKE CLEARS AWAY
AND WE SEE WHERE WE ARE
WE'LL SEE ALL THAT REALLY MATTERS IS LOVE
WHEN YOU GET TO THE HEART

I WISH YOU WERE HERE (OH MY DARLIN')

by Michael Foster

WISH YOU WERE HERE, OH MY DARLIN'
I STILL THINK ABOUT ME AND YOU

OF ALL OF THE PLEASURES I'VE KNOWN IN MY LIFE
THIS ONE KEEPS HOLDING ME NEAR
TIMES THAT WE SPEND IN THOSE INNOCENT DAYS
THOSE WERE THE DAYS YOU WERE HERE

SATURDAY MOVIE, A KISS IN THE DARK
LOVE WAS SO TENDER AND KIND
SIMPLE AND TRUE LIKE THE HEART OF A CHILD
NEVER A DOUBT YOU WERE MINE

WISH YOU WERE HERE, OH MY DARLIN'
SHARIN' THE TIME THAT WE KNEW
WISH YOU WERE HERE, OH MY DARLIN'
I STILL THINK ABOUT ME AND YOU

TIME GOT AWAY WITH THE BOY IN MY FACE
I KNOW IT'S JUST A LITTLE TOO LATE
I HEARD YOU GOT MARRIED
I GUESS YOU STOPPED CARING
STILL NOBODY'S TAKEN YOUR PLACE

CHEATIN' AND LYIN'
WITH HEARTS THAT STOPPED TRYIN'
THAT'S HOW I'M DOIN' THESE DAYS
I MISS YOU TONIGHT AND I WANTED TO WRITE
HERE'S ALL I WANTED TO SAY

WISH YOU WERE HERE, OH MY DARLIN'
SHARIN' THE TIME THAT WE KNEW
WISH YOU WERE HERE, OH MY DARLIN'
I STILL THINK ABOUT ME AND YOU

LITTLE THINGS

by Billy Barber

OOH, OOH
IT'S THE WAY YOU KISS ME
WHEN WE'RE WALKIN' DOWN THE STREET
IT'S THE WORDS YOU WHISPER
WHEN WE'RE DRIFTIN' OFF TO SLEEP
A CERTAIN WAY YOU TOUCH ME
THE WAY YOU SAY HELLO
BABY IT'S THE LITTLE THINGS
THAT MAKE ME LOVE YOU SO

THE WAY YOU POUR YOUR COFFEE
IN THE EARLY MORNING LIGHT
THE WAY YOU CALL MY NAME OUT
IN THE MIDDLE OF THE NIGHT
HOW YOU SIT FOR HOURS
SINGIN' WITH THE RADIO
BABY IT'S THE LITTLE THINGS
THAT MAKE ME LOVE YOU SO

IT'S NOT THE MEMORIES
OR ALL THAT WE'VE BEEN THROUGH
IT'S NOT THE DISTANT DREAMS
THAT KEEPS ME COMIN' BACK TO YOU
IT'S NOT THE PROMISES
THAT KEEP ME WARM AT NIGHT
IT'S JUST THE EVERYDAY
IT'S JUST THE SAFE AND SOUND
IT'S JUST OUR HOME SWEET HOME

AND WHEN WE'RE OLD AND GRAY NOW
AND THE KIDS HAVE GONE AWAY
WE'RE ALONE TOGETHER
I MAY TURN TO YOU AND SAY
THERE'S SOMETHING I FORGOT TO TELL YOU
AND BY NOW I THINK YOU'LL KNOW
BABY IT'S THE LITTLE THINGS
THAT MAKE ME LOVE YOU SO
WOH, WOH
BABY IT'S THE LITTLE THINGS
THAT MAKE ME LOVE YOU SO

WALKIN' IN THE PARK
KISSIN' IN THE DARK
THE LITTLE THINGS, BABY
MAKES ME FEEL ALRIGHT NOW
BABY, IT'S THE LITTLE THINGS
THAT MAKE ME LOVE YOU
BABY IT'S THE LITTLE THINGS
THAT MAKE ME LOVE YOU SO

BABY IT'S THE LITTLE THINGS
THAT MAKE ME LOVE YOU SO

OZARK MOUNTAIN JUBILEE

by Roger Murrah & Scott Anders

I HEAR A ROOSTER CROWING
IT'S A FROSTY MORNING
I CAN ALMOST SEE THE SIGN
I'M GOING SO FAST I CAN'T STOP
I'M JUST A STONES THROW FROM LITTLE ROCK
HEADING FOR THAT MISSOURI LINE

DON'T NEED A MAP TO GET THERE
YOU CAN GET THERE FROM ANYWHERE
WHEN YOU'RE GOING IN YOUR HEAD
I CAN SEE THE ARMS OUT REACHING
JUST LIKE THE DAY I WAS LEAVING
IT'S BEEN OH SO MANY YEARS

LET ME GET ON THE FRISCO SILVER DOLLAR LINE
TAKE MY TIME
SEE ALL I CAN SEE
FIDDLER ROSIN UP YOUR BOW
WE'LL HAVE OUR OWN
OZARK MOUNTAIN JUBILEE

IF I CAN'T BE A FAV'RITE SON
I'LL BE THE PRODIGAL ONE
'CAUSE I BEEN GONE TOO LONG
OH HOW THE YEARS HAVE FLOWN BY
OH HOW I REALIZED
HOW MUCH OF ME IS GONE

LET ME GET ON THE FRISCO SILVER DOLLAR LINE
TAKE MY TIME
SEE ALL I CAN SEE
FIDDLER ROSIN UP YOUR BOW
WE'LL HAVE OUR OWN
OZARK MOUNTAIN JUBILEE

THE INCREDIBLE OAKS BAND

Nowhere is the consistency with which The Oak Ridge Boys have recorded hit songs more apparent than when they perform in concert.

"American Made" opens the show with a burst of energy, followed by the more laid back "Roll Tennessee River", I Guess It Never Hurts" and "What Are You Doing In My Dreams". The show concludes some two hours later with "Bobbie Sue" and "Everybody Wins". For an encore The Oaks sing a medley of "Leaving Louisiana in the Broad Daylight", "Trying to Love Two Women" and "Y'all Come Back Saloon."

One after another the hits just keep coming, providing the audience with a rollercoaster ride of musical entertainment.

The Oaks' dynamic road show has made the group one of the hottest attractions on the concert circuit. Sharing the on-stage limelight with the four singers is the Oaks Band which consists of: Skip Mitchell, lead guitar; Don Breland, bass; Ron Fairchild, keyboards and mandolin; Fred Satterfield, drums; Steve Sanders, rhythm guitar; and Dewey Dorough, saxophone. The six-man unit has been backing The Oak Ridge Boys since 1981.

Don Putnam

Replaces Will Golden - 5/87

No one is prouder of the Oaks Band than the four Oak Ridge Boys themselves. "I think we have the hottest, kickingest band that anybody has," declares Duane Allen. "It's the most consistant band I've ever heard on stage. They are very, very important to our stage show and to the musical expressions of The Oak Ridge Boys.

Touring and record sales are interrelated. The Oaks bolster their record sales by performing in every major market at least once every year and a half. "This is where our band really comes into play," notes Richard Sterban. "We think the people who buy tickets to see us want to hear our hit records performed the way they hear them at home on the stereo or on the radio. It's important for our band to get as close to that same feel on stage as we have on record. Our band is second to none in this business. They are so vital to what we do and to the success of TheOak Ridge Boys."

Joe Bonsall echoes Sterban's sentiments. "We've never recorded anything that the guys in the band haven't been able to cook on," he adds. "That comes from being fortunate enough to have a very talented band."

Like the four singers, the band members all have their own

favorite songs from the Oaks repertoire. Mitchell and Satterfield both favor "Dancing The Night Away." "I like the way Joe sings it," Satterfield says. "It's a classic song," Mitchell affirms.

Dorough and Sanders list "Bobbie Sue" as their favorite tune. Sanders "likes the beat," while Dorough grins and explains, "it got me the job."

Fairchild prefers "I Guess It Never Hurts To Hurt Sometimes," because "It's not a straight country tune." Breland's favorite Oaks' tune is "I Want To Make My Life With You." "It makes a positive statement about life, similar to other songs the Oaks have done," he reasons.

The Oaks Band exhibits the same pride in its music as the four singers. They are very much a part of The Oak Ridge Boys' musical family.

Don Putnam

Don Putnam

RON CHANCEY

As the "Fifth Oak", record producer Ron Chancey is the man behind the studio scene for The Oak Ridge Boys. He has been at the controls since 1977 when the group released its first album for ABC/Dot Records (now MCA Records) entitled "Y'all Come Back Saloon."

It was Chancey who found the album's title track while listening to songs for the group to record. The song reached Number Three in the country charts, thus becoming the Oaks' first successful single release.

His importance as an integral part of the Oak's team is amplified by the fact that every album he has produced for The Oak Ridge Boys has earned a Gold Record (sales of 500,000 or more), with two of them, "Greatest Hits I" and "Fancy Free", reaching Platinum status (sales of 1,000,000 or more).

Chancey and the four Oaks have maintained the ideal producer-artist relationship. "We started off comfortable with each other, and it's still like that," he says. "We never have any cross words, which is unusual to have cut as many albums as we have. Everybody is real relaxed and just rolls with the flow."

Don Putnam

As producer, Chancey also screens much of the material submitted to the Oaks. He is enthusiastic about this facet of his job, although he admits it is a challenge to find just the right songs to record.

Since all four of the Oaks sing lead vocals on different tunes, Chancey must listen for four types of songs, keeping in mind each singer's unique vocal qualities. Each Oak has sung the lead vocal on at least one Number One record.

"Duane is the technical lead singer of the group," Chancey explains. "He sings the real soft, pretty ballads. Joe sings the high-energy type songs. William Lee's songs are the more raw, earthy-type songs. It takes a real special song for Richard to sing. Good bass songs are hard to find."

Chancey explains the Oaks' recording process: "We lay out the basic musical tracks, and one of them will get out there and sing the song just to get the feel and the key right. Then we go back and work on the vocals with all four of them until we get them right."

There are several songs which Chancey believes have been significant in the development of the Oaks' recording career. " 'Thank God For Kids' always does something to

Don Putnam

Don Putnam

people," he says. "And that song really established Golden as a lead singer. 'Dream On' did the same for Richard."

"Of course, I'll always love 'Elvira', but as far as the creative part and the production, 'I Guess It Never Hurts To Hurt Sometimes' is my favorite record. It's the classic recording from a producer's standpoint."

Although it is difficult to pinpoint precisely what makes an Oak Ridge Boy song, Chancey always listens for songs which lend themselves to harmony. "We do songs that have a big chorus, so we can get back to that basic Oak sound." he says. "We may get away from the standard instrumentation, or the production might be a little bit different, but anytime you have these four guys singing together you're going to have their sound."

While many recording artists change producers virtually from one album to the next, The Oak Ridge Boys have kept their winning combination intact with Ron Chancey. Without the "Fifth Oak" their sound just wouldn't be the same.

THE RECORDINGS

Room Service

Together

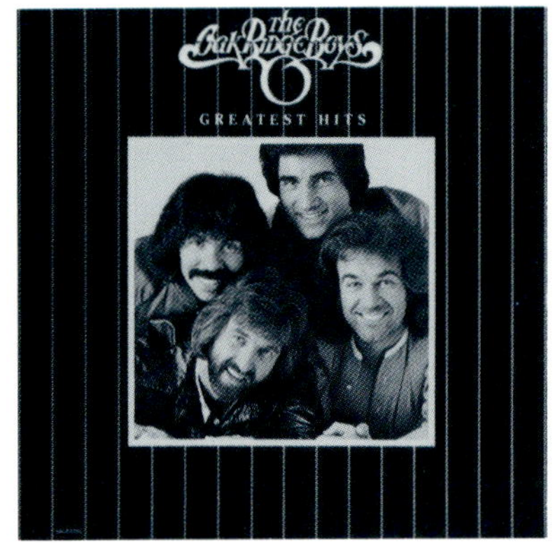

Greatest Hits

Greatest Hits 2

Christmas

Deliver

Step On Out

Soon to be released . . . THE OAKRIDGE BOYS SEASONS

THE MUSIC FOLIOS

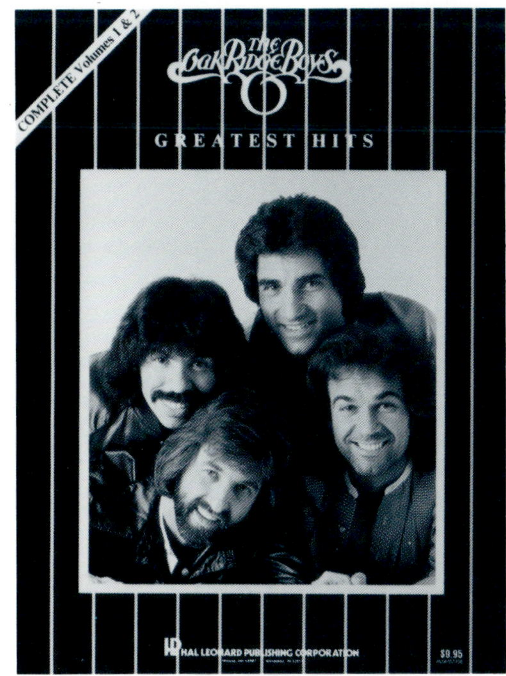

Greatest Hits
Volumes 1 & 2 Complete

Christmas

Deliver

Step On Out

THE OAK RIDGE BOYS
INTERNATIONAL FAN CLUB
329 ROCKLAND ROAD
HENDERSONVILLE, TENNESSEE 37075

Soon to be released . . . THE OAKRIDGE BOYS SEASONS